CW01052159

The Arab World

Glenn Myers

Authentic
LIFESTYLE

Copyright © 2005 Glenn Myers

First published 1998 by OM Publishing
Second edition 2005 by Authentic Lifestyle

Authentic Lifestyle is an imprint of Authentic Media
PO Box 300, Carlisle, Cumbria, CA3 0QS, UK
and PO Box 1047, Waynesboro, GA 30830-2047 USA

09 08 07 06 05   7 6 5 4 3 2

The right of Glenn Myers to be identified as the Author of this Work has been
asserted by him in accordance with Copyright, Designs and Patents Act 1988.

British Library Cataloguing in Publication Data
A catalogue record for this book is available from the British Library

ISBN 1-85078-282-2

Designed by Christopher Lawther, Teamwork, Lancing, West Sussex.
Cover design by Adrian Searle and Sam Richardson.
Typeset by Profile PPS Ltd, Rewe, Exeter, Devon
and printed and bound in Great Britain by Printpoint, Bradford, W. Yorks.

CONTENTS

Start here ...

This book is a broad-brush introduction to the main trends in the Arab World that affect Christian life and witness.

It's based on many interviews with people actively working within, or for, the Arab World, along with a trawl through some of the printed sources and other media.

Thanks to the many people who invested variously in this project. Almost all those I interviewed like to keep a low profile in the Arab World and so I won't name them here. I hope they, and the peoples of the Arab World, see some fruit from their work.

I'm grateful to Arab World Ministries for providing photographs. Thanks also to Knox Haggie and Margaret Beasley for help with translation; to the editor of the Paris-based newspaper *La Croix* and to Christine Mallouhi for permission to use extracts from their publications; to Patrick Johnstone, John Bardsley and their research team whose resources, and ideas, I have borrowed; and to my wife Cordelia and our children.

I hope any criticisms of the Arab World that you may find here will be read as they are intended: for prayer and towards better cross-cultural understanding. I'm not into finger-wagging comparisons with the West. All cultures, western or Arab, have inherent greatness, and are fallen, and need transforming through the gospel.

NOTE ON TERMS

The map shows what we mean by the 'Arab World': strictly, we mean the 'Arabic-speaking world'. Many people who speak Arabic and live in the region would rather we didn't call them Arabs: many Scots who live in the UK and speak English would rather we didn't call them 'English' for the same reason – they aren't. My apologies for the shorthand.

I have also used these terms:

- Christian (meaning any member of the Christian communities of the Arab World, Orthodox, Catholic, or Protestant. As explained in Chapter 6, by no means all of these would lay claim to a living relationship with Christ)

- North Africa (meaning Algeria, Libya, Mauritania, Morocco, Tunisia and Western Sahara)

- The Fertile Crescent (Egypt, Iraq, Israel, Jordan, Lebanon, the Palestinian areas, Sudan and Syria)

- The Gulf (Bahrain, Kuwait, Oman, Qatar, Saudi Arabia, the United Arab Emirates and Yemen)

- The Middle East (the Fertile Crescent plus the Gulf).

And thanks to the regular team who have been in on this project from the outset: my colleagues at WEC International in the UK, my publisher Jeremy Mudditt and my wife and children.

Glenn Myers
November 2004

– 1 –

In the beginning

IT'S IN THE BLOOD

If you're from the Arab World, Christianity is in your blood.

It's hard to believe, but seventeen centuries ago, multitudes of Christians lived among the peoples of North Africa and the Middle East. If you had travelled around the southern Mediterranean in, say, the fourth century AD, you would have been walking through one of the great heartlands of Christianity.

By that time the Church in North Africa and the Middle East was already:

- *Ancient:* the book of Acts tells us that 'Libyans' and 'Arabs' were among those who responded to the first Christian preaching on the day of Pentecost.[1]

- *Influential:* Carthage in Tunisia and Alexandria in Egypt were (along with Rome) the leading cities of the Christian world. They were home to the most influential writers and theologians after the apostles themselves: Clement, Tertullian, Origen, Augustine.

- *Popular:* As early as the third century AD, Tertullian, writing in defence of Christianity, could declare, 'We are a great multitude, almost a majority in each city.'[2]

- *Widespread:* The gospel travelled deeper into North Africa and the Middle East than ever Roman rule did. Relics of church buildings, for example, have been found in North African villages too remote for Roman records.[3] The Christian faith progressed in the Gulf, into Iraq, and down the Nile far into what are now Sudan and Ethiopia.

- *Brave:* It was a church that had produced many martyrs – for example, a young mum named Perpetua, gored by wild animals in the persecution under Emperor Severus in 203; the bishop Cyprian, beheaded in 258. (When Cyprian was sentenced to death – to give us some idea of the spirit of that early North African Church – the Christians in the crowd shouted, 'Let us go and be beheaded with him!' and had to be restrained by troops.)[4]

THE FALL

Yet it fell from all this.

Many of the problems were self-inflicted. The North African Church, which collapsed most completely, was plagued with division. (Not for nothing has the North African Church been called 'The home of uncompromising Christianity.'[5])

Then came the Vandals. Burning, looting, pillaging, this Germanic tribe ravaged North Africa in the early years of the fifth century. Theoretically a Christian people, Vandals subscribed to a heresy called Arianism and brutally attacked the existing Church. Some leaders were exiled or enslaved, others tortured and killed. It was a decapitation of the Church far more effective than anything attempted by the Romans.

A century later, the Byzantines, the successors to the Romans, regained North Africa and imposed on it their alien, Greek-speaking Eastern Christianity. They created some wonderful Christian North African architecture, but, evidently, not much else. By the seventh century, Christendom in North Africa was an unpleasant thing to behold: broken, dispirited, heresy-prone, at war with itself.

In the Middle East, churches survived better – partly because Christian liturgy and literature were translated into local languages (this never happened in North Africa or the Gulf), and partly because churches were spared destruction at the hands of the Vandals.

THEN CAME THE ARABS

During the middle of the seventh century the Muslim armies famously burst from Arabia. Within a hundred years of the Prophet's death, barely pausing for a few brotherly spats, Arabs had swept all over the Middle East and North Africa, to the heart of Asia (one tradition says even to China), across Spain and deep into France. That they even turned back there was probably due to disinterest, rather than military defeat.

It was a dazzling series of military conquests, greatly helped by the divisions in the Christian world at the time. Then the Arabs followed military victory by constructing a great new civilization.

They unified into a single empire, with a single currency, an area from Central Asia to Western Europe: the first time this had ever been done. Trade between East and West flourished. Prosperity grew and with it, fine cities. Cordoba, Fez, Tunis, Cairo, Damascus, Baghdad became the great cities of the western half of the world. Innovation and new products flowed west: Indian numerals (we call them 'arabic'), cotton, rice, sugar-cane and citrus fruits. Our English names for fine fabrics date from the Muslim empire: muslin, damask, gauze, mohair, taffeta.

The Muslim empire took the best of Greek science and philosophy (getting it translated into Arabic first by Syrian Christians), and then built on it to become the leading scientific and technological power of the day: disciplines like medicine, pharmacology, astronomy and astrology thrived in Muslim hands. Paper-making arrived from China. Great buildings were erected: per-haps most audaciously of all, the Dome of the Rock on the Temple Mount in Jerusalem, the world's most uncompromising architectural statement. A Muslim male citizen of this empire had rights and freedoms the equal of any man anywhere on earth at that time. It was (breathe it softly) the United States of its day, a civilization with supreme energy and vision, the global superpower, rivalled only by China.

PEOPLE MOVEMENTS TO ISLAM

Islam was at the heart of the new order. And, though it did not happen quickly, individuals, family groups and whole tribes began converting to the new faith.

There are plenty of good reasons as to why this happened.

- Early Islam was brash, confident and used to winning. It had good reason to be: so far (despite reverses in battle sometimes) it had always eventually come out on top.

- It was open and attractive (or, at least, its open and attractive elements were ascendant). Here's al-Kindi (*c.* 801-66), father of Islamic philosophy:

   We should not be ashamed to acknowledge truth from whatever source it comes to us, even if it is brought to us by former generations and foreign peoples. For him who seeks the truth there is nothing of higher value than truth itself.[6]

   Other Muslim writers felt free enough to argue even that reason should be given a higher place than revelation.[7] (Arab writers have been stabbed for less than that in today's Arab World.)

- It was tolerant: Christians and Jews worked for the Muslims and for the most part lived together well.

RELIGIOUS TOLERANCE, NOT WHAT IT USED TO BE

Jerusalem was captured by the Arabs in 638. 'Under Muslim rule, Christian churches and populations were left unmolested … Jews, long banned from living there by Christian rulers, were permitted to return, live, and worship in the city of Solomon and David.'

Then the First Crusade happened and 'five centuries of peaceful coexistence were now shattered by a series of holy wars which pitted Christianity against Islam and left an enduring legacy of distrust and misunderstanding'.[8]
– *John L Esposito*

- It was simple: as Kenneth Cragg has pointed out, here was a faith that could be expressed in fifteen syllables – much to be preferred to the dense fog that was Christian theology at the time. (Is Christ two natures welded together or one fused into an amalgam? Your salvation depends on getting the answer right.)[9]

  Even the apparatus of the new religion was simple and minimal: compare the spartan elegance of the mosque with the busy, glittering, smoke-filled, gold-inlaid Byzantine basilicas.

- It was Arab and Middle Eastern, not Greek. It boasted a holy book in Arabic. It put the Arabs, not the Jews, at the centre of the theological universe. It answered Semitic problems of money, marriage, dowry, inheritance, not Greek concerns like the Nature of Being.

- To many of the tribes accepting Islam, it seemed only to require a few outward changes. They could retain their animist beliefs for the really important issues in life: whom to marry, how to fend off curses, how to make your fields fertile.

- (And not to be forgotten) It was a way of paying less tax, avoiding discrimination, and improving your promotion prospects.

It was a slow progress. By the end of the eighth century – after a hundred years of Muslim rule – fewer than 10% of people in places like Iraq, Syria, Egypt, Tunisia were Muslim. Two hundred years after that, it is not certain that Muslims were in the majority anywhere in the world outside Arabia itself.[10] It was slow: but the trend was clear.

ISLAM CONQUERS ALL

As the centuries passed, dynasties rose and fell; Arabs lost their empire to Turkic speakers; but the Islamic colouring seeped ever deeper into the fabric of the Middle East and North Africa.

Tolerance for Christians also declined (partly in response to the Crusades and to what Christians began to do to Muslims and Jews in Spain). In North Africa, for example, in 1159 the Muslim reformer Abd el-Moumen gave what remained of the Church in Carthage the choice of conversion or death.[11]

Much more commonly (though not all the time nor everywhere with the same zeal), Christians and Jews were discriminated against because of their faith. As well as paying the poll tax, they couldn't marry Muslim women; couldn't wear certain colours; weren't allowed to live in ostentatious buildings; couldn't extend their churches or synagogues. Their word in court had less weight than that of a Muslim; and they could be excluded from political power.[12]

Islam grew stronger and stronger. Between the tenth and thirteenth centuries, for example, the Muslim empire faced enormous challenges: civil strife between the Sunni and Shi'a parts of Islam; campaigns by the western Crusaders; attacks by Mongols from the East. Sunni Muslims won all three: taming the Shi'as, crushing the Crusaders, converting and assimilating the Mongols.[13]

By the fifteenth century, the ascendancy of Islam in North Africa was complete. Further East, the ancient churches turned inward, grew isolated from each other, lost converts to Islam, but – despite all – endured.

It was possible as a Muslim[14] in the sixteenth century to look across the world with quiet satisfaction. True, there had been setbacks. Spain and Sicily, for example, had been reconquered by western Christian kingdoms. The Islamic

> **OOPS**
>
> The Ottoman emperors administered the rival Orthodox Christian patriarchies in their domains under a single patriarch, based in Istanbul. Attaining this office became the source for much unholy behaviour. Kenneth Cragg reports that there were 31 different patriarchs during the century from 1595. 'In 1726, Callixtus III paid 5,600 pounds in gold for his appointment and died the following day of a heart attack.'[15]

empire was split into an Arabic-speaking Sunni bit and a Shi'a bit centred on Iran (both parts were ruled by Turks). In neither part were the empires, nor their many squabbling rulers, as authentically Islamic as a purist might have liked.

To the south and east were pagans who may well turn to Islam in time. To the north and west, the Christians were a greater threat, but, again, the Islamic empire had recently captured Constantinople, Serbia, Bosnia-Herzegovina and Albania, and was working on further European expansion. Not for nothing were contemporary European observers calling them 'the present terror of the world.'[16]

For almost its first thousand years, on the whole, the fortunes of Islam had followed the theological script. Islam, The Straight Path, was conquering all.

Unfortunately (for them), it didn't stay that way.

– 2 –

Downhill from here

Somewhere in the seventeenth century the history of the Islamic lands started to come unstitched. For a thousand years the Islamic worldview had been woven together with all that was best in religion, science, and civilization. Now, as if some Old Testament prophet had spoken against it, the political and economic supremacy of the Islamic lands was challenged and overcome.

The successful challenger wasn't Christianity. It was modernity, or  Westernization, that evolving collection of cultural elements that the peoples of Europe were shortly to dump onto the world. Europe's increasing strength in population, capital, innovation, statecraft, and economic and military power was not matched by the peoples of North Africa or the Middle East.

Here are some of the milestones:

- In 1683 the Ottoman Turks, heirs to the Islamic Empire, and global superpower of the day, began a siege of Vienna that seemed to threaten the security of all Europe. Later the same year they were decisively beaten back. A peace treaty in 1699 settled the matter. The world had changed. A contemporary (Ottoman) writer recognized the hugeness of what had happened:

    This was a calamitous defeat, of such magnitude that there has never been its like since the first appearance of the Ottoman state.[17]

    From that date until 1923 (when it disappeared altogether) the Ottoman Empire shrivelled in size and influence.

- Sometime during the seventeenth century, it became cheaper to carry spices from the Far East to Europe by sea rather than overland through Cairo; the lucrative trade slipped from Arab to European hands.

- In 1774, the Ottomans, defeated by Catherine the Great, handed over control of the Crimean Tartars to Russia. This was the first time that a Muslim people in their empire had been yielded over to European sovereignty.

- Trade with the Ottomans made up 50% of all French trade in the late sixteenth century; it fell to only 5% by the eighteenth; it was 10% of all British trade in the mid-seventeenth century, 1% a hundred years later.[18] The loss of market share reflected a technological and economic stagnation.

- Europeans had the good fortune to be living amidst supplies of wood, water, and coal which they harnessed for their new industries to great advantage; North Africa and the Middle East had none of these. (A mysterious substance called petroleum leaked from the ground sometimes but no-one had much use for it.)

- European populations rose fast (for example, Britain's went from 16m to 27m in the 50 years to 1850); the population in the Middle East and North Africa remained much the same.

- In 1830, the French landed on the North African coast and occupied Algiers. At first they sought only to provide a stable environment for their merchants. But soon they were running the country, and shortly after that, populating it with French settlers. A millennium earlier it had been the Arabs who were conquering and settling.

- By 1850, Egypt was selling all its raw cotton to Britain for processing; Bedouin tribesman were buying shirts made in Lancashire. Fabrics (and all kind of high-value-added goods) were now being shipped from Europe to the Arab World, not the other way.

- Between 1854 and 1879 the Ottomans borrowed large amounts from the Europeans and on unfavourable terms. By 1875 they could no longer keep up with payments. In 1881 foreign creditors were running large parts of the Ottoman government.[19]

At the end of the First World War the loss was terminal. The victorious European powers, armed with maps and pencils, redrew the boundaries of the Arab World. A line was sketched across the British-mandated territory of Palestine to create Jordan. Part of Saudi Arabia was stuck onto the edge of Iraq. To make up the loss, a piece of Kuwait was cut out and sellotaped onto Saudi Arabia. The French helped themselves to Lebanon and Syria.[20] For a people who had been 'the present terror of the world' only three centuries earlier, this was a humiliating moment.

Worse was to follow.

A FRESH START

The following years promised much by way of fresh starts for the Arab World, but delivered little. Nationalism brought independence, but resulted in a dreary succession of one-party states. The discovery of oil brought fabulous riches to some, boosted the spread of Islam around the globe, but in the end led to a greater economic dependence on the rich countries. The Iraq wars of 1990-1991 and (especially) 2003 only reinforced a humiliating reality: the independent Arab nations must endure the unendurable arrogance of the world's current superpower.

The stubborn fact of Israel highlights all this Arab failure like graffiti on a new state monument. A UN resolution opened the way to the creation of a Jewish state in 1948. Its presence pushed Arabs from their homes with what felt like another flourish of the colonial pencil. In the face of Arab hostility, Israel went on expanding its territory through a series of wars. The Six-Day War in 1967 saw a combined Arab attacking force humiliated dreadfully as Israel grabbed Sinai, Jerusalem, the Palestinian part of Jordan and the Golan Heights from various Arab countries.

Historian Albert Hourani says of this Arab disaster:

The defeat of 1967 was widely regarded as being not only a military setback but a kind of moral judgement. If the Arabs had been defeated so quickly, completely and publicly, might it not be a sign that there was something rotten in their societies and in the moral system which they expressed?[21]

An Arab psychologist concluded:

The 20th century will be remembered in the collective Arab memory as a period of failure and humiliation. High hopes were raised of a great Arab revival at the turn of the century following the collapse of the Ottoman Empire. Hopes of a great cultural and political awakening were raised again following the discovery and exploitation of oil. But as the century ends, the Arabs find themselves as weak and dependent on outside powers as when it began, if not more so.[22]

It continues today. The ongoing story of Western and Israeli domination, and perceived Arab subjection, is the continuing agony of the Arabs, and one of the great fault-lines in the world.

WESTERNIZATION AS A WAY OF LIFE

Beyond the economic and political stories, Westernization as a collection of ideas, or a set of symbols, is now the greatest challenge to the cultures of the Middle East and North Africa – quite as compelling as Islamization itself was to pre-Islamic cultures 1300 years ago.

It is an influence felt everywhere. Historian Bernard Lewis has pointed out that even hardline anti-Western states such as Iran claim legitimacy for themselves by appealing to Western standards of statehood:

The state still wears a Western coat and hat in the form of a written constitution, a legislative assembly, and some form of elections. All these were maintained in the Islamic Republic of Iran, though there is of course no precedent for them either in the ancient Iranian or sacred Islamic past.[23]

Popular culture is dominated by mass media, which in turn is also dominated by Western images and products. In some Middle Eastern cities, you can choose from up to 80 TV channels. It is very hard to find a single house in Cairo that doesn't have a TV, even if it is only a black-and-white one powered by an extension cable from a neighbour's electric point.

Surveys show that even if almost no-one can be found in the Arab World supporting American foreign policy, a majority want American-style democracy.[24] This people-pressure is slowly squeezing Arab governments: Algeria's (rather flawed) general election of 2004 was nevertheless perhaps the Arab World's freest and fairest yet. Though sales of American colas plummetted as a protest against the 2003 Iraqi war and subsequent occupation, sales of local colas ('Mecca cola', 'Zam Zam cola') thrived. America may be out, but cola and democracy are in.

THE SCANDAL

This Westernizing force puts a strain on Islam and the Arab World. Ordinary, moderate Arab-world people believe, with justification, their families to be more decent, more together and more honourable than their counterparts in the West. They are more God-fearing, their daughters more modest, their communities more cohesive. With good reason, ordinary Arabs are proud of their culture, its generosity, its hospitality, its honour.

Yet the secular, immoral Western world has greater economic clout, snazzier technology, better military toys, and the decisive influence on the world stage.

It isn't right. Though the colonizers have departed, Arabs have almost have ended up with *dhimmi* status[25] in their own lands – tolerated by the West but culturally, economically and politically brushed aside. This – understandably – seems like a scandal, a world upside-down.

Think of the words that are almost sacred in Arab cultures but scorned in the West:

- Chastity
- Decency
- Shame
- Respect for elders
- Honour for parents
- Obedience to the family
- Tradition

The painful dilemma facing the Arab World is how to stay true to these values while being buffeted in the West's dehumanizing gale. The variety of responses on display include rejecting westernization, rejecting the Arab World completely, and trying to steer some middle course.

- Here is the reason for the rising popularity of Islam across the Arab World since the 1970s.

- Here is also why people join Al-Qaeda, or embrace other forms of radical Islam, some violent, some non-violent. They feel Arab and Muslim honour is at stake, and has been lost, and they want it back. Suicide bombs are honour killings.

- Some people emigrate physically; some 'emigrate' emotionally, adopting what they imagine to be the lifestyle of the West without actually leaving the Arab World.

- Some escape into all the kinds of escapisms we're familiar in the West, shopping, TV, drugs, mysticism.

- A few become Christians.

- And most people, of course, like most of us, simply muddle through all this moral incoherence as best as they can.

THE CHALLENGE

This history and present reality – what does it mean for Christian witness?

- Our view of the Arab World is confused by all the wrong images. Arabs and Westerners share a long history of mutual misunderstanding. The Biblical texts are apt: 'The man who thinks he knows something doesn't yet know as he ought to know,' and, 'knowledge puffs up, but love builds up.'[26]

- Our westernness (for those of us who are from that part of the world) severely complicates the task of presenting Christ. We do not arrive as neutral actors. Our crusading, colonizing history and current bossy practice is quite reasonably resented. And our morals are suspect. When we initially enter the Arab World we are like the girl with the shortest skirt at their party: a curiosity perhaps, an object of fun for some, but hardly the person to seek out for spiritual counsel.

- To make any kind of progress, Christians need to demonstrate Christian love in a cultural language that Arabs, Muslim and Christian, understand. This calls for all kinds of unusual, un-Western choices: wearing veils, giving away our possessions, being lavish with our hospitality and time, assiduously paying our social debts. Only then, clad in Arab World dress, will the gospel be seen for what it truly is.

- We need a spirit of humility, suffering, learning and love. Christine Mallouhi, drawing on long and intense cross-cultural experience, gives an illustration:

Sometimes I think Westerners are replacing grace and the Holy Spirit by a 'spirit of teaching'...

It would be an interesting exercise to examine the prospectus forms submitted by candidates [for missionary service] and note how many intended coming to 'teach' or 'disciple'. They would be the majority. Now let me tell you about Ed. He is a successful professional family man who in mid-life decided to give his talents to sharing Christ's love in the Muslim world. Before his family left for the field he told a national Christian, 'I don't have any specialized training in theology or Islam. I don't know that I have anything to teach. I just want to be a friend to Muslims and love them for Jesus.' The national Christian, embracing him with tears in his eyes said, 'Ed, we have been looking for you for years.'[27]

– 3 –

Arab Worlds today

A SELECTION OF ARAB WORLDS

As foreign Christians wanting to learn about the Arab World we could be forgiven for already feeling out of our depth. And this is only Chapter Three. The tangled history of encounter between Arab World peoples and Westerners, entwined with the sorry story of Christian/Muslim relations, much of it sticky with blood, is a great challenge.

Yet we also have to consider the complexity of the 'Arab World' itself. This is a rich and diverse place. Whether we look at regions or peoples, at wealth and poverty or city versus traditional life, we find a host of 'Arab Worlds,' each one calling for a different expression of the gospel.

THREE REGIONS

It's possible to map out three broad regions within the Arab World: the Gulf (Saudi Arabia and the surrounding countries), the Fertile Crescent (the countries from Syria and Iraq in the north to Egypt and Sudan in the south) and North Africa (everything west of Egypt). The three regions contrast sharply:

- The Gulf is rich, solidly Muslim, and rather hostile to indigenous Christian witness and presence. But many expatriates, some of them Christians, also dwell here.

- The Fertile Crescent is home to almost all the Arab World's Arabic-speaking Christian community, church groups that have lived here since Christ's apostles established them. The region has long traditions of peaceful coexistence between Muslims, Christians and Jews. Recent decades of radicalism–Islamic, Jewish and Western–have brought severe strains.

- North Africa is more Muslim than the Fertile Crescent – Christians are isolated here – but more like the edge of the Arab World than its centre: many of its people would claim to be Berbers, not Arabs. Some are aware of a pre-Arab, Christian past.

The Arabic-speaking family of peoples also spreads far beyond the countries of the Arab World: south into West Africa, and north into Europe. You can also find descendants of Arab trading communities as far away as Sri Lanka.

MANY PEOPLES

Then, when we look at the tribes and peoples of the Arab World, we see yet more complexity. Some of the main groups:

- *Bedouin*. The original Arabs, known to the Bible. Here are the supreme exemplars of the strict desert tribal codes: lavish in their hospitality to strangers, chivalrous and chauvinistic, generous with their possessions  and friendship. Islam was born among them. They are its chosen people; God spoke in their language. Bedouin of various kinds still populate the Arab World, though fewer and fewer of them are nomads these days. You could distinguish two main clusters – Arabian and Saharan – and numerous sub-groups.

- *Arabs*. Arabic-speaking descendants of the peoples who intermarried with the Bedouin over the centuries. These people form the bulk of the 'Arab World': Arabs of the Fertile Crescent and the Gulf, Egyptians, Sudanese Arabs, Yemenis, Libyans, Arabs of North Africa.

- *Berbers*. These are peoples of North Africa who still retain their own non-Arab ethnic identity. Again they exist as many separate tribes speaking related but different languages – for example: Kabyle Berber (Algeria), Riff

Berber (Morocco), Saharan Berber (all across Egypt and North Africa), Shawiya Berber (Algeria), Shilha Berber (Morocco), Tamazight (Morocco).

- *Arabic-speaking peoples of the sub-Sahara:* Descendants of Arabs and Berbers. Though Muslims, the faith of most of these may perhaps fairly be described as 'animism with a light dusting of Islam'. Among these people are the Tuaregs, the famous blue-veiled nomads of the Sahara, and the Hassaniya (or Moors) of Mali and Niger. Sudan is an Arab World country by some measures, but Arabs are actually in the minority here.

- *Minority peoples.* A few small tribes in the Fertile Crescent belong to the Arab World but have long resisted both Arabization and Islamization. For example, the Druze are heirs to a mystery religion, into which you only may be born, not converted. The Assyrians of Iraq and Syria have retained a Christian and non-Arab identity to this day. At the last count, there was a tiny community of just 650 Samaritans–descendants of the Samaritans of Jesus' time – in two cities in the West Bank.[28]

Other groups could be mentioned but are beyond the scope of this book:

- *Jews.* In Israel but also in many Jewish settlements in Arab World cities as far apart as Casablanca and Damascus.

- *Expatriates.* Many groups, particularly from south and south-east Asia and Western countries. They actually outnumber local Arabs in some Gulf coun- tries. Some maintain a Christian witness despite the many restrictions.

- *Indo-Iranian peoples.* Peoples like Iraqi Kurds and Iraqi Persians speak lan- guages unrelated to Arabic or the Berber languages, tend to be Shi'a rather than Sunni Muslims, and culturally are much closer to the peoples of Iran, Pakistan and Afghanistan.

Do the stats and you find that of around 285 million people in the countries of the Arab League, perhaps 200m are actually Arabs.

WEALTH AND POVERTY

A landmark study by Arab economists in 2002 brought out some more textures within the Arab World. Here are some:

- The Arab World spans the full range of 'human development' (as measured by economists, that is). Some of the small Gulf Arab countries are up with the richest countries in the world in their standards of living. Some countries – Egypt, Saudi Arabia, for example – rank in the middle of the human development league. And some (Yemen, Mauritania, Djibouti) prop up the bottom of the table.

- The Arab World stands out as having what the economists called three key deficits. It is politically the least-free part of the world (this is the 'freedom deficit'). Only sub-Saharan Africa provides less opportunity for the female half of the population (the 'women's empowerment deficit'). And then there's the 'human capabilities/knowledge deficit': the Arab World has 5% of the world population, but only 0.5% of the world's internet users, it produces only a few dozen films a year, it has few novelists and translates fewer than 350 books a year into Arabic (five times that number are translated into Greek, for example). Similar figures confirm the wretched state of Arab-inspired science and technology, research, and entrepreneurship. Adult literacy, at just 62% is much worse than the global average of 79%. The Arab World is 'more rich than developed', with its wealth arising from the sands, not from the creativity or industriousness of its people.

How can the Church tailor its mission to the Arab World in the light of all this? Let's look at a couple of main areas.

THE RURAL POOR

By far the largest group in the Arab World are the poor. Half the people of the Arab World live in villages; typically they work as farmers, herders or craftsmen (sometimes all three).

They share the lot of the poor around the world. Often they lack access to education, health care, decent housing, and literacy. If they survive childhood, they marry young, produce large families, and die before their time. People who happen to be female, young, or mentally or physically handicapped, suffer particularly badly. For example, five million mentally handicapped people live in the Arab World: fewer than 50,000 are in any programme of formal care.

A number of Christian-based charitable operations like hospitals and clinics perform remarkable service in the rural Arab World. These are stressful and lonely postings: some people have been murdered by extremists, others bombed or threatened. And they are not allowed to use words to explain the gospel. But they are nevertheless bringing something of the fragrance of Christ to rural Arabs, and opportunities and options for overseas Christians to serve are, if anything, increasing. At the time of writing there are exceptional opportunities to serve in Iraq and help rebuild a nation shattered by war and dictatorship. You know the gospel is coming when outsiders come to the Arab World not bringing body armour, helmet, and gun; nor a suitcase of samples for sale; nor even a sheaf of discipleship materials; but a towel and a basin.

> **GET AWAY FROM IT ALL**
>
> Most afternoons Yemeni men chew the young, tender *qat* leaves. After completely filling their cheeks with *qat* – a 1-2 hour process – there is a brief high followed by a long 'mellow' phase. The effect can last well into the night. It is not an exaggeration to say that all of Yemeni society revolves around *qat*, especially in the north ... it also effectively partitions society into those who chew *qat* and those who don't.[29]

THE URBAN POOR

For still another Arab World, and for even a greater challenge for the Christian Church, look at the masses of young men idling in coffee shops, walking around the streets, reading newspapers, looking for work in the great cities.

Arab World populations have far outstripped the capacity of cities to accommodate them properly. One urban wage and apartment, for example, are sometimes shared between a dozen or more family members.

The young urban masses of the Arab World feel the combined heat of all the smouldering troubles of the region: unemployment, population growth, poverty, the challenges and provocations of the alien Western world. Life is tough and unfair. These are people who have studied hard – done their best with what they had – and yet have nothing to show for it. Many despair of ever earning enough money to rent an apartment of their own or get married.

A few turn to Christ. Most of the 100,000 or so Arabs who are currently involved in Bible Correspondence Courses, for example, are the young, literate, urban poor. The thousands each month who contact Arabic evangelistic websites like www.maarifa.org also come from this group.

So, of course, do the Islamic radicals who have seized the world's headlines since September 11th 2001.

As a group, the young urban populations of the Arab World stand out: they are the future of the Arab World. They are also at the centre of all its troubles, all of them victims of injustice, all of them convinced of the need for radical change in the Arab World.

Who–or what–will win their devotion and their passion?

- 4 -

The heat is turned up

If the 9/11 terrorists wanted to make an impact, they surely succeeded.

America was humiliated. Wars started. Governments fell. Many have died in events that are still unfurling. Further turmoil and instability presumably lie ahead.

Terror, however, headline-grabbing as it is, destabilising and murderous as it is, famous though it makes the terrorists, heartening though it is to those who hate America and the West, isn't the central issue facing the Arab World's masses. Even if terrorists manage to compile some event that actually outstages 9/11 – destruction of Saudi oil infrastructure would be interesting, for example – that will remain true.

Every society has its crazies: the second greatest homeland terrorist attack on America (we recall), the Oklahoma bombing, was perpetrated not by a Muslim from the Arab World but by an all-American white male.

The signature issue for the Arab World is the perceived, dire, unreformed state of the Arab World when compared with almost everywhere else, and especially with the West. Every economic statistic, every high-handed military act by Israel or the Western world, and much of the difficulty and frustration of every day life increases the sense of shame and anger. The sense – as an Old Testament prophet might put it – of being the tail, and not the head, feels personal and causes deep loss of honour.

We note in passing that some perspective is also important here. More compelling even than the pain and confusion of the current time are the daily issues of living. The Arab World may be in a ferment, but you still have to put bread on the table. Only the very rich or the unemployed have, in general, time to ferment. A survey in October 2002, interestingly, showed how much ordinary Americans and ordinary Arabs actually shared common values. Most put work and family at their top of the things they really worry about, with foreign relations or geopolitics way down the list.[30]

SHAKEN AND STIRRED

How, then, has 9/11 and all that has followed, changed the Arab World? The short answer is that the events have intensified trends already present – turned up the heat. However much, and in whatever directions, the Arab World was being shaken and stirred before 9/11, it is now being shaken up and stirred rather more. The activity is in many conflicting directions.

Here are some.

1. DENIAL AND BLAME-SHIFTING

Surely the most depressing and useless response of all, denial is nevertheless a clear trend.

Gallup polls in February 2002 revealed a widespread belief across the Arab World that Arabs were not involved *at all* in 9/11. It was the Israelis or CIA agents who had really flown the planes, playing some complex, anti-Arab games. Kuwaitis were the worst deniers, with 89% of them denying any Arab involvement in 9/11.[31]

The extent of denial of reality in the Arab World is constantly a shock to out-side Western observers. Until his death in 1999, the most senior Islamic scholar to advise the Saudi government, Sheikh Abdel-Aziz Bin Baz, believed and taught that the earth was flat.

A close cousin to the outright denial of the completely obvious is the tendency to blame everyone else for the Arab World's problems. The unrolling centuries have of course brought on many candidates: the Mongols, the Crusaders, the French and British, the Arab nationalist dictators, the Americans and the Jews.

In all this, our Muslim friends surely have grounds for expecting our forbearance and friendship.

2. RADICAL ISLAM

Radical Islam remains an option for a minority. It isn't new. It has a long history as a purist stream within Islam:

- Some date it to a thirteenth-century martyr named Ibn Taimaiya, who was unwise enough to suggest that the newly converted Mongol rulers were not living according to the Qur'an.

- In the eighteenth century, at almost exactly the same time that John Wesley was establishing Methodism in Britain and the United States, a reformer named Muhammad ibn Abd al-Wahhab was returning Muslims in central Arabia to the strictest of the four Islamic schools of law. He made an alliance with the ruler of a small market town, Muhammad ibn Saud, to form a state that lived under this Islamic law. From those beginnings sprang the state of Saudi Arabia – a state today best understood as made up of a rich ruling family who have prevented their own overthrow by letting their Wahhabist Muslim critics run the religious life of the nation.

- In the twentieth century the writings of Sayyid Qutb inspired generations of radicals. He understood the Qur'an as teaching violence against both non-Muslims and bad Muslims. A majority of Muslims would reject Qutb's take on the Qur'an but he is a source for the whole radical Islamic family. Some groups focussed on (as they saw it) purifying the Arab World. Others, like Al-Qaeda and its children, declared holy war first on the Communist world and then on the West to free the 'Islamic nation' from their influence. Having ended Communism (in their understanding) they are now trying to bring down the West.

Probably the real attraction of the radical Islamists lies not in the precision or otherwise of their Qur'anic exegesis but in the eloquence of their paranoia and attraction of their call to martyrdom. Here's Osama bin Laden in February 2003:

> *What is happening in Palestine is a small sample of what will take place in the [entire] region: the killing of men, women and children; imprisonment, terrorism and the destruction of houses; the pillaging of the land and razing of factories; and putting the people into a perpetual state of fear, where they can expect death at any time from a rocket or shell destroying their houses and killing their womenfolk.[32]*

Terrorists (if they don't die in suicide attacks) have been known to mellow. In (non-Arab) Iran some of the most dangerous student radicals from the 1979 revolution were some of the staunchest supporters of moderate reform a quarter of a century later. Radical Islamic terrorism will wax and wane in influence. But as long as the Arab World experiences severe injustice and powerlessness, there will surely be a ready supply of new suicide bombers.

3. REPRESSION AND REFORM

A third trend since 9/11 is that of governments harshly repressing known or suspected terrorists or dissidents, while at the same time taking baby-steps to real political reform.

Most Arab World governments have tended to take it for granted that you can generally lock up whomever you wish for as a long as you like, in the name of 'national security'. The events of September 11th and Islamist acts of terror in the Arab World itself, have only strengthened this urge.

...at the same time, optimistic observers detect the much-delayed arrival of democratic structures in Arab countries. Many countries are setting up experiments in democratic participation. It remains to be seen if these tender shoots are real reform, or (as the pessimists suspect) just a harmless diversion.

Both the repression and the reform, of course, are responses to the public rage against their governments that has been present for decades but has been intensified since Sept 11th.

4. MODERATE BACKLASH

A fourth trend (and the major one) is of Arab people rejecting radical Islam and scrabbling to find other ways forward for the Arab World. This too has been a feature of the Arab World for decades, but has a new urgency at the moment.

You can observe a 'moderate backlash' of people who are fed up of the radical Islamists but still angry with the West, and with the Western-oriented elites who run their countries.

The day after al-Qaeda bombed Jewish targets in Casablanca in May 2003, killing 45 people (all Muslims), hundreds of thousands of Muslims came out onto the streets, waving banners saying things like 'say no to hate'. More than a thousand members of the Jewish community felt free enough to join them. Some other examples of the 'moderate backlash':

• *Moderate Islamic political parties*. The Arab World's little splashes of democracy of recent years have been a positive force to create new forms of Islamic politics. Whereas political Islam in the 1980s and early 1990s was about revolutionary overthrow, the Islamist parties today tend to be more moderate – they have to be, they have discovered, if they want power. When radical Islamists were elected to a Jordanian embryo parliament in 1989, they found little popular support, and were ousted a year later.

Turkey is not an Arab country, but its Islamist-based government is an interesting example from elsewhere in the Muslim world. It has become far more concerned with sensible politics like social justice and fixing the

economy than headscarves and beards. (Of course it had a head ⌐
much of the rest of the Muslim world: Turkey has a long tradition ⌐
ular state.)

Algeria's military annulled an election in 1992 that would have ushered in
a radical Islamist government, but were happy to let Islamist parties fight

(and as it happened, lose) the
2004 elections. In Egypt, many
former Islamic terrorists have
publicly renounced violence. In
Saudi Arabia in 2004 a famously firebrand preacher has had a
similar public repentance.
Political Islam is becoming
moderate, constructive and
mainstream.

- *Islam as a personal faith*. Another trend is for forms of Islam that are much
  more concerned with personal life and problems than with the reform of
  society. Egypt, the leader in this as in so much in the Arab World, has
  Islamic televangelists like Amr Khaled and Khaled al-Guindi (this latter runs
  a dial-a-*fatwa* line). Hugely popular, they are offering an Islam loosened
  from the old legalism and prescriptions, a kind of 'middle class' Islam.[33]

- *Sufism*. Still popular is this time-honoured movement within Islam that is
  internal and mystical rather than external and legalistic. Some Sufi poetry
  contains expressions of longing after God that you would be hard-pressed
  to find bettered in religious writing anywhere. Interestingly, a
  disproportionately high percentage of Muslim-background Christians were
  Sufis once.

- *Conservative values*. Not all these moderating trends are in a direction the
  West would call progressive. Many people, while rejecting violent and radical Islam are espousing the kind of traditional conservative Islam that,
  they claim, was the trend in the first 300 years of Islamic history. They are
  more open to innovation and learning than the radical Islamists, but still
  suspicious of modernizing trends, especially feminism. Indeed, the
  approach to feminism will be a defining civil war within Islam, one that has
  still largely yet to take place.

- *Setting aside.* Another characteristic response – just as has happened with Christianity or perhaps Christendom in the West – is the quiet discarding of Islam. This does not usually mean outright apostasy. Instead, faith is, as it were, consigned to the attic, not for everyday use, but to be brought out only for special occasions like festivals, births, marriages, and deaths.

- *Turning to Christ.* Compared with the other responses listed above, this is a tiny ripple of response, not fit to be called a trend. But it does fit with the broad picture of people trying to find a non-violent, life-affirming, non-secular response to the current squeeze. And since it is our job to track down such mustard seeds of Christianity, we look at it in a bit more detail below.

THE FERMENT AND THE GOSPEL

Why are all these reponses to 9/11 important for the prospects for the Christian gospel? Here's why:

1. They have brought a fresh urgency to the encounter between the Arab World and the world outside, and especially the West. Aside from the angry headlines and acts of violence are many new initiatives for conversations and joint actions between Christians and Muslims. Christians from all over the world should welcome every opportunity for dialogue and peace-making with open arms and great enthusiasm.

2. The house of Islam within which the Arab World has lived for many centuries is widely recognized as needing drastic renovation. In a faith where 'innovation' is regarded with deep suspicion, this is quite a change. These are yeasty, unpredictable days for Islam. In a sense, Islam has never been this way before. Here is a quote from a popular apologist for Islam, Ziauddin Sardar:

The overall consensus amongst Muslim scholars is that the Muslim world is in urgent need of new thought which:

1. Liberates tradition from fossilized history and transforms it from a suffocating into a life-enhancing enterprise.

2. Formulates a new fiqh *– that is, a new jurisprudence and law,* *focussed on contemporary needs, requirements and issues ...*

3. Reopens the 'gates of ijtihad' *[innovation] and leads, through reasoned and sustained struggle, to a fresh understanding and renewed comprehension of the teachings of the Qur'an and the life and traditions of the prophet Muhammad.*[34]

For centuries, the main impression to outsiders has been of an Arab World that was closed to new ideas – a victim perhaps of its own greatness, but nevertheless a world that the rest of the world passed by, pausing only to siphon off some oil.

The heat of modernity and post-modernity, the loss of honour, the suffering at Western hands, the disgust at terrorism in Islam's name, have come together like a storm rattling the windows and roof of the house of Islam, and blowing doors open. It remains to be seen exactly how the Arab World is remoulded over the coming years and decades. What seems very likely, amid the upheaval, is that tiny flowers of Christian faith will find room to grow.

Next we look at two Arab World countries that have been unusually destabilised in recent years, to see if we can trace a Christian story there.

KILLINGS IN BETHLEHEM

The following is not intended as the definitive comment on the Israeli/Palestinian conflict: it's a one-sided observation of a multi-faceted tragedy. There is, indeed, a kind of madness on both sides. But I'm including it to help show something of the depth of pain the conflict causes in the Arab World.

Saturday, October 27, 2001

Bethlehem, Palestine

I want to bear witness today to what I have seen in Bethlehem this week. What I am reporting to you is not more political propaganda to trump one cause over another. It is simply a record of a few of the events taking place this week. It is up to you to make sense of them and explain them to yourselves and others.

At least 22 people from Bethlehem have died in the past 10 days. The current cycle of killings began on October 18th with the assassinations of three young men who were on Israel's 'wanted' list. Any death is tragic, but those of us who live elsewhere are usually able to read about such deaths from the newspaper over our breakfast and shrug them off as the unfortunate but unavoidable price of conflict.

However, the stories of the 19 others who died this week, and the events surrounding them, are deeply disturbing, and force us to look deeper into the reality of the Palestinian experience under occupation. I can tell you a few of these stories first hand.

On Friday, October 19th, Musa George Abu Aid, 19 years old, was shot in his living room standing next to his father, and collapsed dead as his father stood helplessly. An Israeli sniper could evidently see shadows through the living room window curtains. Identities were not important to the shooters.

On this same day a young mother in a village just south of Bethlehem had gone into labor and was experiencing complications. Her husband put her in the car and tried to rush her to the hospital in Jerusalem. He was blocked by Israeli soldiers at the checkpoint near Rachel's tomb in Bethlehem and refused permission to pass. Despite all his desperate pleadings they maintained their refusal as precious time slipped away. His wife, Marian Suboh, 28, and her unborn child died waiting for hope.

On Saturday, October 20, a young 17-year-old boy named Johnny Thaljiah was walking across Manger Square at noon. If any of you have come to the Church of the Nativity as a pilgrim in the past three years, you may have met Johnny. He would often sit at the entrance to the Church and hand out scarves or other covering for those who wished to enter the Church but were inappropriately attired. An Orthodox Christian, on this day he had just been at worship with his family in Nativity Church. He was carrying the baby of one of his cousins, trying to make the baby laugh.

Less than 100 feet from Nativity Church, he was shot by an Israeli sniper from a hill nearly a mile away. Johnny gently lay the baby down on the stones of Manger Square and then fell over dead. Johnny was not on anyone's 'wanted' list. He was a Christian worshipping with his family in the oldest Christian church in the world.

We do not know why Johnny was chosen as a human target. But the snipers are very good. And their equipment was the very newest and best sniper rifles U.S. tax dollars could buy. They had good success.

Later that day Rania Elias Kharofah, a 22 years old Orthodox Christian and a mother of two young children, convinced her husband that she should drive to get food because it might not be safe for a man. While on her way to the store she was shot in the arm by sniper fire. She got out of her car and took refuge in a shop. An Israeli tank approached the shop and all the people in the shop ran out into the street. Rania, wounded and unable to run, tried to crouch back in a corner and hide. The tank shelled the shop and covered it with machine gun fire. Rania was later found dead with multiple bullet wounds.

Also on Saturday Eisha Abu Ada, 39, and a mother of 8 children, left her family in Jerusalem to go to Bethlehem and visit her parents to see if they were safe and to seek to provide anything they might need under the siege. This brave, devoted daughter was shot by a sniper bullet in her parents' yard.

On Sunday, October 21st, Muhammad Baraga, 30, a deaf person, was shot by Israeli soldiers in front of his home because he could not hear their orders to him.

At first we heard all these reports in disbelief, but by Friday were able to drive around Bethlehem and see much of this damage with our own eyes. And the killings continued. On Wednesday, October 24th, Issa Jalil el-Ali, a 55-year-old Catholic Christian who was the father of five, was hit by a sniper bullet bringing food home to his family. His wife was in the car beside him but could do nothing as he died. Sami Awad and I attended his funeral at the Church of the Nativity on Thursday. During this day, 39-year-old Salama al-Dibis, the father of nine children, was killed by sniper bullets at the front of his house. On the afternoon of Friday, October 26th, 28-year-old Faras Salahat was joyfully running last minute errands in preparation for his wedding that very night. He was shot by sniper fire and the families gathered for the wedding feast attended his funeral the following day.

One last story. Today, Saturday, October 27th, Sami Awad and I went to visit the father of Johnny Thaljiah, the young boy killed in Manger Square one week ago. After sharing his grief for a time, he asked us to go with him to attend another memorial service taking place in Manger Square for several other young men killed during the week. More than 100 people had gathered in the Square, representing many families from Bethlehem, to express their grief and share their condolences with the families of the dead. As the service was in progress, suddenly five or six shots whistled over our heads across the Square. People began running for cover in various directions, mindful that Johnny had been killed in the Square in just this way.

Sami and I began walking across the Square with Johnny's father, heading back to his home. When we got near the spot where Johnny was killed another volley of shots was fired over the Square. Then Sami pointed to one of the crosses on top of the Church of the Nativity. This time their target was a lighted Orthodox cross on the roof of the Church. From a mile away, and at the angle they were shooting, this was an extremely difficult target. But the expert snipers managed to hit the center of the cross with several shots.

Bearing witness from Bethlehem,

– Robin Wainwright, Holy Land Trust USA; Sami Awad, Holy Land Trust Palestine.[35]

– 5 –

Case studies

Algeria and Sudan – two very different countries – share some features in common. They are both:

- Somewhat on the fringes of the Arab World
- Are suffering or have suffered an unusual amount of turmoil at the hands of the radical Islamists
- Have a growing, suffering, Church

ALGERIA

In 1988, riots in the streets of Algiers prompted the government to introduce more democracy in the former French colony. The Islamist party, the FIS, won the first, local council, elections in 1990. The FIS were strong nationally, their charity work was impressive, they stood for God and tradition ('and how can we vote against God?' people asked). Most of all, people wanted a change.

Not much happened after this first election. Mosque preaching became a bit more radical. Qur'anic texts replaced the 'Socialist Republic of Algeria' signs over Algerian council buildings. The Islamists started neighbourhood watch schemes, applying pressure to women who dressed too skimpily, or men who smoked tobacco or hash.

In 1991, after much debate (should men vote on behalf of their wives? Or should women be allowed their own vote?), Algeria went to the polls for a national government. The FIS were the clear leaders after the first round. The government, citing the FIS's well-trailed intention to rewrite the Algerian constitution, which would have once more shut the door on democracy, undemocratically annulled the elections and outlawed the FIS. As many as 20,000 people were interned.

Then the killings started: Islamists attacking the symbols of government and of Westernization; government forces trying to curb the Islamists. The FIS splintered. And from that time, through the next several years, Algeria spiralled bloodily out of control.

Artists, journalists, politicians, unveiled women, Catholic missionaries: the toll of bodies grew. By the mid-1990s, ten thousand a year were being added – their throats slit, or their bodies hanged from trees, or left, charred, in burnt villages.

ENTER THE CHURCH

Caught in the midst of this, softest of targets, were the overseas Christians - mostly French Catholic missionaries. When the history of the 20th century Christian Church is written, a special chapter ought to be devoted to Algeria's Catholic missionaries. However much Protestants and evangelicals may disagree with Catholic theology, we have much to learn from their Christian response during this nightmare period in Algeria's history.

'Why do we stay?' asked the bishop of the Algerian city of Oran, Pierre Claverie, in a sermon six weeks before losing his life to a car bomb in August 1996.

Because of Jesus, there's no other reason. We have no interests to protect, no influence to preserve. This is not a kind of perverse masochism, or suicidal tendency. We have no power; instead, we are there as at a sick friend's bedside, holding his hand tightly, or wiping his forehead ... Isn't it essential for a Christian to be there in places of suffering and abandonment?

Where would we look for the church of Jesus Christ, the very own Body of Christ, unless we first looked there? I believe the church is dying because it is not close enough to the Cross of its Lord. It seems paradoxical, yet Paul demonstrates so clearly, that its strength, its vitality, hope and productivity, all flow from there.

'We're a living a kind of *kenosis* with the people of Algeria', declared the Prior of seven Trappist monks, borrowing a theological term more usually used to describing Christ's emptying of himself to become a vulnerable, suffering servant. Having abandoned all the trappings of colonial power, he suggested, they were seeking to be Christlike in suffering alongside the Algerian nation. (Another Catholic missionary has used the phrase 'blood brothers of the Algerians'.) All seven members of that Trappist community were later martyred.

After the deaths of four members of another Catholic order, the White Fathers, in 1994, one bishop commented, We are letting ourselves be exposed to the violence that is hitting many in Algeria ... Nobody can decide beforehand to be martyrs. We decide ahead of time, that we will endeavour to be faithful to the people God has given us to serve, and to love.'

IMPACT OF A LIFE WELL-LIVED

A letter published in the local press after the assassination by Islamists of four Catholic White Fathers, in Algeria, December 26th, 1994.

Farewell friends ... From today, like many others in Kabylia, I feel like an orphan. For many of us, [the White Fathers] were our family, a refuge, an enormous moral support. All those who used to go to them to pour out confidences, to ask advice, feel very alone; a deep sorrow is closing in on them.

With enormous courage, they stayed among us, for the sake of all who needed them. We all want to pay them our respects.

I want to say to their loved ones and to their many friends how much I feel for them. They were the kind of people who cannot just belong to one small family.

To the parents of our youngest father, Christian, if it can help you, I have this to say. You should know that in his last few days, Christian was very happy. He was bubbling with joy, for he had succeeded in getting off the ground a project which he was really keen on – to build a library for the young people ...

These, our fathers, are no longer here physically. Their memory will stay alive among us. They are examples to us of courage and self-sacrifice. Right up to the last moments, the doors of their hearts and their homes remained wide open.

If they were still able to speak for themselves, I am sure they would tell their killers: 'God forgive you, and have mercy on your souls!'

I am sure that from the place where they are now, they carry on praying for peace and brotherhood in our dear Algeria, which they have loved so much.

– Signed by: 'a young Algerian girl who wishes them to rest in peace, and who promises to follow in their path'.

THE CONSEQUENCES

The major consequence of the past several years is that Algeria's experiment with Islamism seems to be at an end: people appear fed up of Islamist politics. Deeper, the affair with the Islamists has left turmoil in many hearts. A French Catholic journalist put it this way:

Horror reached out and touched everyone in the name of Islam. And you began to hear it said: 'But this isn't Islam. Not our Islam. Where in the Qur'an do we read about such crimes?'...

Algerians are in search of a new God. This would be expected from intellectuals ... But it is more surprising to see 'the debate' about Islam taking place at the heart of many Algerian families.

Some read and re-read the Qur'an, or ask a learned son or uncle to explain this or that sura of the Qur'an, or search each 'Hadith' (sayings attributed to the Prophet).

Others ask question after question, on other faiths, in particular on Christianity, so as to know whether Christians have been through similar troubled and bloody times.

Others still – there are few but you can find them – are so scared by their own religion becoming unrecognizable to them, that they are near apostasy. You can see some reading the Bible. In doing so they are trying to 'stay close to Allah, even if he is not Allah'. They are 'in search of a God, since they can't live without him, but a God of love and goodness, a 'God for a Democracy', as they also call him.

This is the least of the religious paradoxes thrown up by the bloody struggle being fought between those in power and the Islamist groups.

SUDAN

Sudan may offer similar clues to the rise, and paradoxical fruit, of Islamism. The radical Islamists took over the country in a military coup in 1989.

They have continued a long war with the south – a centuries-long conflict that has its roots at least as far back as the Middle Ages, with northern Arabs raiding and plundering slaves from the south and west.

It's a war that sometimes dies down, only to be fanned into flame again by some new turn of events. By 2004 the latest civil war had clocked up 20 years, and was showing signs of exhaustion. Obervers of the region were gloomy however. As long as the Northern Arabs wanted an Islamic state and also wanted this state to be united with the non-Muslim, populous, and oil-rich south, peace would be elusive.[36]

Sudan's president, Hasan Omar al-Bashir, is making attempts to end Sudan's international pariah status, with talk of democracy, development, and national reconciliation. But the government is still captive to radical Islamist zeal, even though it has dumped its chief Islamist ideologue, Hasan al-Turabi, in an unbrotherly spat. 'Sudan will carry the torch of Islam to all countries, even your own,' the head of a Sudanese Qur'anic school told a Christian journalist interviewing him for a documentary.[37]

Human rights groups continue to tell a story of amputations, mutilations, floggings, enslavement and forced conversion. There are mass-killings of non-Arabs by Arab Islamist militias known as the *janjaweed* in joint operations with the army.[38] Women are still flogged and fined for not wearing a headscarf.[39]

Under the rule of the radical Islamists, Sudan has put out a welcome mat for all the evils of the world: ethnic conflict, child soldiers, army brutality, slavery, starvation, poverty, murder, ignorance, persecution. Al-Bashir's government gives permission for the UN to take aid to the south of Sudan, then has been known to drop bombs on the aid conveys.

THE CONSEQUENCES

Sudan is like no other Arab country in that its southern third (in terms of population) is a mix of animists and Christians who have never been Muslim. These people waged a long war with the radical Islamist government, and also have a terrible record of human rights abuse.

Somewhere within all this turmoil, however, is a story yet to be fully told. The Sudanese Church is isolated from the rest of Christendom. Yet some claim that the Church has grown from 15% to 70% of the Southern population since the 'holy war' began in 1992. The Church of England has grown from half a million when the British left in 1955 to five million now, supported by several thousand Sudanese clergy (there were only half a dozen in 1955).[40] Other churches are showing similar startling expansion.

Some of the four million people displaced by the conflict have started churches elsewhere in Sudan; people deprived even of basic medicines have seen remarkable healings in Christ's name.

The *Jesus* film (a dramatization of Luke's gospel, now the world's most widely-screened film) has had an estimated total gross audience of 50 million in Sudan.[41] Even allowing for many repeat viewings, this equates to a sizeable proportion of Sudan's 33m population seeing the film – some in the Muslim Arab North as well as many in the African south. A very reliable source has personally counted half a million people turning to Christ in that land over recent years. Some people claim that if there were religious freedom in Sudan, many more Arab Muslims would publicly turn to Christ.[42]

WHERE SIN ABOUNDS ...

These two examples – from the two countries in the Arab World that have suffered the most Islamist conflict – show us:

1 When violent Islamism is let loose on a country, chaos, death and disillusionment follow.

2 The suffering of the Church (along with that of the rest of the country) can be intense.

3 In the two countries we have looked at, disillusion with the Islamists, coupled also with the heroic suffering of the best of the Christians, has led many people to wonder which way to turn – and a number have turned to Christ.

You could almost say from these two examples – surely it doesn't happen everywhere – that the more Islamism manifests its violent self, the brighter the Christians shine and the more the Church grows. Where sin abounds – at least sometimes – grace abounds even more.

For the Christian communities of the Arab World, then, these are unusual days of danger and opportunity. We look at these churches in more detail next.

– 6 –

The Church

STRUGGLING

Struggling is a good one-word summary of the Christian Church in the Arab World.

It is, overall, declining. And the decline has accelerated in the past decades. Former Anglican Archbishop George Carey made a special point of supporting overseas Christians under persecution and has said:

> *If present trends continue, in the not too distant future the original heartland of the gospel could well become a kind of 'Christian theme park,' where the only Christian witness will be by tourists visiting the holy sites.*[43]

Here's an estimate of what has happened to the percentage of Christians in various countries since 1900:[44]

	1900	2000
Iraq	6%	1.6%
Egypt	18%	13%
Syria	15%	5.1%
Jordan	6%	2.8%
Lebanon	67%	32%
Palestine/Israel	10%	2.1%
Total Middle East	19.4%	7.5%

Emigration to the West is the great cause of the decline. Three quarters of all the migrants from Lebanon and Egypt are Christians. Half of all the Arabs now residing in the United States are Christians.[45]

Conversion to Islam (especially from among the poor) is another reason. As many as 15,000 people from the ancient Christian communities may be turning to Islam in Egypt each year.[46] The difference in relative birthrates between the two groups is still another factor.

MISFITS

Arab Christians are regarded as an embarrassment by many Arab Muslims, despite all that the Christians have done to identify with their own nations and people.

Consider, for example, the problems of being one of the tiny Arab Anglican community in Israel. They hold Israeli passports (with all the problems that brings) but are not Jews; they are Arabs, but not Muslims. They are not Eastern Christians (because they belong to a Western denomination). And Western Christian visitors tramp past their church doors in Bethlehem and Nazareth, in search of authentic Christian sites, without so much as saying hello: not much fellowship there either. No wonder their community is in decline (in spite of an increased number of ordained clergy and a bold attempt to address the complex issues).

A MIXTURE

As everywhere in the world, not all the parts of the Arab World Christian community bear fruit to Jesus. Many are simply traditional adherents to Christianity.[47] A few from some Christian communities have been implicated in terrible massacres. Some are terrorists. 'The Middle East,' an experienced Christian worker said to me, 'is home to the best, and the worst, Christians in the world.'

So who are the Christians? It may be helpful to look at three overlapping categories:

- The ancient churches
- The Anglicans and Protestants
- The Muslim Background Believers (MBBs)

THE ANCIENT CHURCHES

You can count three families of Orthodox churches and several flavours of Catholic Church spread through Iraq, Syria, Lebanon, Jordan, Israel, the Palestinian areas, and, above all, Egypt and Sudan. As well as Arabs, you can find small peoples who have resisted the Arabizing impulse for many centuries: peoples like the Armenians, the Assyrians, and the Chaldean Christians.

Christians worldwide ought to be proud of these churches. Like some stubborn old grandad who has refused to die, old-fashioned, set in their ways, they have continued to remind the Arab World of its bright Christian past.

They have endured much persecution. Possibly no denomination has supplied so many martyrs, over such a long period of history, as the Coptic Orthodox Church.

Yet they have stuck with the Christian faith. Many of them, indeed, believe that their ceremonies and liturgy (so strange to Western perceptions) carry echoes of the original Christian worship in the temple courts, which in turn borrowed from the Jewish temple worship itself.

They count the great Fathers like Athanasius and John Chrysostom as their own. Some of their theology warms the heart of those of us who are evangelicals (though many Orthodox would consider us heretics).[48] Here's a snippet from an Orthodox systematic theology:

'Making redemption ours' means the acceptance, wholeheartedly and with gratitude, of the redeeming work of Christ on behalf of the sinner so that he can truly be saved.[49]

Here's another:

> For [a person] to make [justification, being put right with God] his own
> and the inalienable property of his life, not only it but all the benefits
> which flowed from the Sacrifice of Christ the Saviour on the Cross, he
> must accept and make it his own and retain it all his life within himself
> with ardent faith.[50]

Eastern Christians have risen to positions of great influence in Muslim societies. Back in the early centuries of Islam, when Islamic influence was centred at Baghdad, Christians were important administrators, translators, pro-
fessionals, and traders. They are still so today. You can find Eastern Christians
in high government positions in countries across the Fertile Crescent. One
was UN Secretary-General for a term.[51]

And the Christians of the Fertile Crescent have developed ways of coexisting
with Islam, and cooperating to build their societies, that are quite different
from the characteristic European responses. Christians the world over can
learn from this, as an Anglican bishop from a Muslim context observed:

> Historically there have been three different ways for Christians to deal
> with Islam ... the Western crusading response; the response of Eastern
> Byzantine Christianity, which was to heap abuse on Islam; and ... the
> response of the large numbers of Christians who actually lived in the
> Muslim world and helped to create what we call Islamic civilization. It is
> getting more and more important to find people like that, and there are
> fewer and fewer of them about.[52]

Declining and struggling though they may be, the ancient churches – and
especially the Orthodox – live on as a significant Christian presence in the
Arab World.

THE PROTESTANTS

A look at the Protestant Church in the Arab World also reveals signs of
struggle. There are wonderful Christians, leaders, ministries, and churches in
the Protestant part of the Arab World. Praise God for them. Protestant
churches are growing (slowly). But they also suffer under pressures that

would squash most of us. Here are some:

- Protestants are so few in the Arab World – perhaps seven for every thousand people. Strip out the Sudanese Christians from these figures (who belong more properly to sub-Saharan Africa) and the Protestants in the Arab World become three in every thousand. That figure includes many expatriates.

- They are not always protected from Islamist pressure by their governments. Fear can dominate, rather than faith. Government regulations and culture make life difficult. (All this is true for the ancient churches too.)

- Relations with the traditional churches are often strained.

- Dependence on Western denominations can lead to theological peculiarities, sectarianism, a lack of self-sufficiency, and a distorted spirituality.

- Trained leaders are few – so are training options. And many young people who opt for overseas training don't come back.

- Support materials like books are expensive, in short supply, and not always relevant.

Don't picture, then, a radiant, victorious Protestant church in the Arab World, bearing witness with the calm grace and simple courage of a Perpetua or a

Cyprian. Some indeed are like that. Think instead of a representative sample – strong, weak and in-between – of your own church flown into the sunshine of the Arab World. Allocate them sparsely: a few in this city, one in that village, two (who don't like each other) in that town. Make the state suspicious, and the law so awkward that it's hard even to register a Christian marriage. Take away most of their friends, books and music. Put a few under surveillance. Arrest one or two. Put a number of them out of work and then send the pastor overseas ...

THE MBBS

The hardest struggle of the lot is reserved for the so-called MBBs (Muslim Background Believers) – people from Muslim families who have turned to Christ. Such people are found in Orthodox, Catholic, and Protestant churches and in none.

To turn to Christ from a Muslim home in the Arab World is, sadly, to set yourself against your family, your nation-state, and your people. Your act shames the people you love the most, slurs the good name of your family, and puts you, and them, under political suspicion. It makes you all a target for the Islamists. It is one of the worst things you can do to your family and every Muslim Background Believer bears the consequences of it throughout his or her life.

No wonder many MBBs live strange, shadowy lives: reading the Bible in secret; staying late after work to meet with Christians; holding church meetings in houses under the guise of birthday parties.

Nor do they find the churches places where their needs are necessarily met. The churches have been betrayed many times by false brothers. New converts are often regarded with deep suspicion or rejected altogether. Even if churches do not reject them, MBBs struggle to fit in and feel at home in what is a quite alien cultural setting.

Many MBBs never quite admit to their families what they are doing. They always have to watch their words and sometimes their backs. For many, emigration is the only solution to an impossible set of circumstances. Of those who stay, some have lost their lives; many have turned back or (in the case of Christian women) been hastily married to a Muslim.

The Church in the Arab World, then, is struggling with one of the most hostile environments to the open profession of Christian faith in the world. If any corner of Christendom deserves our prayers, the Christians of the Arab World, ancient and modern, open and hidden, surely do.

– 7 –

The prospects

What are the prospects for the gospel in the Arab World? Let's look at the bad news first.

THE DOWNSIDE

- Perhaps no region on earth has tangled so much and so badly with 'Christendom'. As we have seen, the decline in Muslim political fortunes mirrored the rise in European and Western ones. Islam is a world-system in which such things matter deeply. Now, the secular cultures of the West, like some acid, are rotting the fabric of Islamic culture.

  Christianity, despite its long history as part of the Arab World, is more associated with the (crusading, colonizing, culture-busting and immoral) West.

- The Church in the Arab World is small, divided, harassed and shrinking.

- The key condition that might let the Church grow in peace – tolerance of Muslims turning to Christ – is remarkably absent in the Arab World. Few things can so unite Governments, radical Islamists, and ordinary, decent

Muslim families as people of Muslim background turning to Christ. In no region of the world is conversion so beset with cultural obstacles and physical danger. Muslim Background Believers' might regard Jesus' words to the early disciples as apt: 'You will be betrayed even by parents, brothers, relatives and friends.'[53] 'A time is coming when anyone who kills you will think he is offering a service to God.'[54]

- Radical Islam, in addition, makes Christian life and witness difficult and dangerous.

It's reasonable, then, to be gloomy about prospects for the Christian gospel in the Arab World.

BUT GOD...

Except that no-one I interviewed felt that way.

Instead, they were excited. Workers who have served Christ in the Arab World for 25 or even 40 years are using such phrases as 'unprecedented openness', 'day of opportunity', 'never seen this before in my lifetime'. According to my informants, these are about the most exciting days for Christian witness in the Arab World in the whole of history.

One explained his optimism by saying, 'The present "congregation" of Arab World Christians look determined to follow Christ through whatever circumstances he allows'.[55]

Here's the perspective of one specialist Arab-World watcher:

> If we compare the Arab Muslim world with a number of other mission fields in the world today, it's very unproductive. However, if we compare what is happening in the Arab Muslim world with what has happened down through history since the inception of Islam, we are in a tremendously encouraging period. We have seen an increasing tempo of conversions and feel that we are approaching more and more that place of real breakthrough in the Arab Muslim world.[56]

These are sober people (for the most part). So what's happening? Many things. Together they add up only to a gentle breeze. But still, a breeze.

PRAYER MOVEMENTS

There seems to be a great increase in the prayerful interest of Christians in the Arab World, and more so since the 9/11 events. This is, of course, rather hard to measure. But local sources attest to it. 'Never before has so much prayer been focussed by so many people in so many diverse places onto one region,' wrote one to me.[57] 'This is an indication of God preparing for something significant to happen.'

MASS MEDIA

It is hard to overstate the importance of mass media, and especially television, in the Arab World. For most, TV is the definitive source of information about the world.

After half-hearted attempts to ban or control satellite TV broadcasts, every country in the Arab World has joined the scramble to get its national voice on satellite TV. Saudi money sponsors any number of channels. Even TV Mauritania, allegedly the world's most boring TV channel, is available via

satellite. Egypt, by no means a rich country, launched Nilesat in 1998 at a cost of $160m, to provide direct TV broadcasts – a project privately admitted to be 'more important to the Egyptian people than bread'. The Qatar-based satellite TV station Al-Jazeera is famous in the West for broadcasting audio tapes of Osama bin Laden and anti-Western propaganda, but has come as a breath of fresh, objective air in the Arab World. (It annoys Arab and Western governments equally.) Some of its programmes attract 50m viewers or more.

In May 1996, broadcasts began of the first ever Arabic-language, Christian satellite TV channel, SAT-7. SAT-7 is an experiment in Christian unity, a channel from and for the Christians of the Arab World.

It's hard to overestimate the potential impact of this one ministry. Now broadcasting 24 hours a day, SAT-7's imaginative mix of programming is proving popular.

Other groups are also providing satellite TV. Algerian Christians, for example, have founded CMA TV which broadcasts in Arabic and Berber.

Slightly older forms of media ministry are also finding receptive hearts. *Magalla*, an indigenous, Christian-based youth magazine is read by approaching half a million people monthly in the Arab World, and sells at major news outlets.

Medium and short-wave radio broadcasts are much cheaper than satellite TV and are vital and well-received. Audience research indicates that one country in the Arabian peninsular, for example, has a regular listenership to gospel radio somewhere between 50,000 (low estimate) and 300,000 (more likely estimate) – astonishing figures for a country with essentially no known indigenous church. And the quality as well as the quantity, of response is increasing. One radio executive told me, 'Twenty-five years ago, of all the letters we received, hardly one in twenty showed any sign of interest in spiritual things. Now, almost every letter does.'

The *Jesus* film has been shown and copied widely around the Arab World. Some countries, notably Iraq, have put it on national TV – this is true of other Christian videos also. (Other countries have banned the *Jesus* film, thereby increasing its appeal.)

Mel Gibson's movie *The Passion of the Christ* was shown in cinemas right across the Arab World. The similarities between Aramaic and Arabic meant that Arabs could understand some of the dialogue without subtitles – unlike the rest of us. The open, public showing of this film in countries where it is difficult sometimes even to bring in a Bible was a remarkable step forward for Christian witness.

The Bible and related material are always prominent and good sellers at the Cairo International Book Fair, the second largest book fair in the world. In recent years, Egyptian Bible Society products have been advertised prominently on the front page of newspapers and on billboards during the fair.

A number of Christian groups present gifts to the thousands of people who migrate annually between North Africa and Southern Europe – typically gospels, Bibles, and copies of the *Jesus* video.

Some websites dedicated to explaining the gospel to Arabs are seeing extraordinary responses. One site run from Finland has a chatroom that needs eight Arabic-speaking Christians working full-time to stay on top of all the conversations.

Arabic Bibles are being downloaded from the Internet. One ministry I know of calculated that, on their own, they were seeing 5,000 Bibles per month finding their way onto hard disks in the Arab World – and each one, of course, can be further copied and shared.

VISIONS AND DREAMS

Another evidence of the gentle outpouring of the Spirit in the Arab World is the number of Arabs who are having dreams about Jesus. Year after year this goes on, common enough to be mentioned even in secular anthropology courses, quiet testimony to Jesus knocking on the door of Arab hearts.

Here is a typical story. In one North African country, a man had a disturbing vision. Later, he had a recurrent dream that someone would come to him who would be white-skinned and who would explain a vision to him. One day, a white-skinned Christian came around to see if he could rent an apartment from this man. They agreed a deal, and the Christian moved in. They became friends. After a while, the landlord shared his story, and ultimately became a Christian himself.

David Lundy, the international director of Arab World Ministries, which places many expatriate Christians in the Arab World, told me, 'Our people come across examples of nationals who have had visions and dreams. So our prayer is constantly, "Lord, keep us from spending time with people who are really not open and will never be open. We have limited time, we work 9-5, even living takes more effort, so we don't have a lot of discretionary time to build friendships. Therefore Lord, lead us to seekers."'[58]

THE RENEWAL OF ANCIENT CHURCHES

The ancient churches of the Fertile Crescent are experiencing renewal and revival. It is widespread though by no means universal.

- After centuries of isolation, the churches of the Fertile Crescent are opening up to each other and to Christians from the outside. The flow of fellowship, the sharing of resources, and the growth in unity are all promoting renewal. It is not happening everywhere, but it is happening.

- The 'Movement for Salvation of Souls' a long-established, indigenous, Biblical movement has impacted the whole Church in Egypt.

- During the 1970s, again in Egypt, there was something of a revival within monasticism, centred around a reforming monk named Matthew the Poor. Out of his influence, many people began seeking God through Bible study, theology, and prayer.

  These people subsequently became pioneering figures in the spiritual renewal of Orthodoxy, teaching the scriptures, for example, to congregations numbering in the thousands. A number of them are now bishops (only monks can become bishops within Orthodoxy). And the renewal continues: 5,000 people gather weekly (for example) in St Mark's cathedral in Cairo to attend a Bible study led by Shenouda III, the 'coptic pope'.

- A prayer movement is gaining strength in Egypt, embracing the whole doctrinal spread of the Church, intent on seeing Muslims turn to Christ. Some people claim this is Egypt's destiny: they like to recall Egypt's history as a previous centre of intercession, in the days of the Desert Fathers, and they refer to a prophecy in Isaiah 19:19 'there will be an altar to the LORD in the heart of Egypt'.

- In places, again in the late 1970s, foreign missionaries did youth work among Christian-background children that has now led to a wider, non-monastic stream of renewed leaders within Orthodoxy. One Egyptian Christian leader has said, 'Long term, the biggest influence that Western missionaries will have had in the past quarter of a century is that they've woken up the local church.'

- Revival has come in some places. Some isolated village Orthodox churches have seen a touch of God without initially knowing that the same things were happening in neighbouring villages. Revival has also stirred some of the Protestant denominations. Thousands of people have been touched – this in the heart of the Middle East. And this blessing has flowed over the walls of the Christian community.

- There has been a sharp increase in the numbers of Egyptian Christian-background people with a vision for sharing the gospel with Muslims, something that was almost unheard of 15 years ago.

- Church groups like the Maronites (an isolated denomination that linked up with the Catholics in the sixteenth century) have experienced renewal in recent years. Taking Bibles to some Maronite communities used to result in stonings: no longer. There are now some outstanding Maronite Bible teachers and a strong and growing community of renewed Maronite Christians.

QUESTIONS IN THE GULF

The Gulf States remain the ones with the least visible Christian presence. Yet even here, things are stirring. It's perilous to put too much into print, but it is clear that, by various means, many people from the Gulf States are becoming interested in the gospel.

Saudi Arabia is a case in point. We saw it in Chapter 4 as an uneasy alliance where a wealthy, Westernized elite have kept the Islamists happy by giving them a free hand to control the religious elements of national life. Flowing from this are the religious police; the banning of Christian symbols, meetings, and books; the harsh laws ... and the distinct lack of popular enthusiasm for Islam. In Egypt, they have to close streets because the mosques are full for Friday prayers. That's not a problem in Saudi Arabia. And from Saudi Arabia come many letters and emails from people hungry for a different way. Upheaval in Saudi Arabia is bound to come sooner or later. Watch out for little churches appearing shortly afterwards.

CHURCHES IN NORTH AFRICA

This has already happened in North Africa. In the past decade, real churches of local people from a Muslim background have emerged all across North Africa. Excluding Libya, each North African nation – Morocco, Algeria, Tunisia, and even the remote desert state of Mauritania – is home to at least a handful of indigenous Christian congregations.

An international prayer movement was organized on behalf of one of these countries in 1999. In the years since then, the Church in this country has grown from a few score Christians to a few hundred, and from no congregations of churches to several. Pre-1999, conversions usually involved lot of expatriate involvement; since 1999, the friendship of local believers became decisive. And some people claim that in this country as a whole, a materialistic and rather disinterested society has become more open, more questioning, and more hungry.

Since Christian life in all these lands fizzled out somewhere in the first half of the second millennium, this represents a significant comeback for the Christian faith.

THE EXAMPLE OF ALGERIA

The movement is most developed in Algeria. Earlier we described Algeria as the country in the Arab World (perhaps along with Sudan) where the Islamist pressures have been at their most violently destructive. It turns out that Algeria is also the home of what may turn out to be a people movement out of Islam.

In Algeria's Kabyle mountains are a set of villages occupied by Berber tribesmen. As many as 75% of all Algerians would claim to be Berbers[59] (30% speak a Berber language). They are interesting for several reasons.

For one, they were reluctant converts to Islam. An ancient Muslim historical record describes them apostasizing a dozen times before they were finally subdued. They have always resisted colonial pressures (Roman, Arab, Turkish, European) and so this is perhaps not surprising.

Second, their version of Islam has more in common with folk religion than textbook Muslim belief: a religion of charms, magic, the evil eye, and holy people and places. This folk Islam – the religion of the rural poor throughout the Arab World – is anathema to the radical Islamist. So the fierce rise of radical Islam causes much of the rest of Muslim world to shake and strain under the pressure. ('This Islam is not our Islam.')

Third, the *Jesus* film and the New Testament have recently been translated into the Kabyle Berber language – the first film and book ever produced in this language. Radio and now satellite TV broadcasts, also in Berber, are received there.

Fourth, bizarrely, Berber folk memory retains distant images of a semi-Christian past. Some examples of many that could be cited:[60]

1 During the Feast of Eid, when the sheep is slaughtered (an Islamic custom), women wipe up some blood from the sheep with a handful of earth and daub it on the doorposts, explaining that if evil passed that way, this would protect them.

2 When someone is very ill, it is a tradition, when everything else has been

tried, to haul him through a hole in the roof: a memory, perhaps of a gospel story.

3 After dressing a baby a mother in some places makes the sign of the cross over the child with her forearms, twice, to protect him.

4 A newborn baby will be placed in its cot next to the animals, because it is believed that a newborn among animals is blessed.

5 Mothers will sing a lullaby using the name of Jesus, believing it to protect the child.

A Christian movement has developed in Kabylia that is more advanced than among any other group of Muslims in the Arab World. Every village has a Christian presence. Converts already number at least in the thousands. If you turn to Christ, it is likely you will already know someone in your extended family who has become a Christian before you. The churches pray and fast and expect conversions and miracles; they are the kind of churches that have grown rapidly elsewhere in the world during this century. Thirteen of them, so far, have successfully registered with the authorities – congregations of Algerian Christians.

I asked two Berber leaders what problems their Church faced. 'All of Kabylia isn't converted yet,' they replied. (They perhaps might have mentioned that the churches are short of leaders, and that many of the Christians are new and young in the faith, and that the fight for political recognition has only just begun. How can Algerian Christians raise their children in the Christian faith, for example, when the schools assume everyone is a Muslim?)

CONCLUSION

In human terms, the odds are stacked against the Christian Church in the Arab World. Yet it is not hard also to find oddly confident Christians and Christian workers, full of faith and excitement for the future. Some clearly believe that the future of the Church in the Arab World is bright – even brighter than its distant past. What will happen? It is perhaps yet to be shaped. We need to watch (and pray for) this space.

RESOURCES

NEWSPAPERS

I strongly recommend you read some Arab World newspapers in English; it's fascinating, humbling and enlightening, and much better to go straight to the source than to read things written by outsiders. Even if the newspapers only reflect some, rather than all, strands of Arab opinion (those of English-speaking middle class elites) they are enormously valuable. Here are three I particularly liked: search engines will reveal more.

www.arabnews.com
From Saudi Arabia

www.metimes.com
Independent Middle Eastern coverage

weekly.ahram.org.eg
Internet version of an Egyptian English-language newspaper.

Not a newspaper but also fun to visit is al-Jazeera's English news internet site:

English.aljazeera.net

BOOKS

An avalanche since 9/11, with more coming out all the time. Here a few gems, that I think thoughtful Muslims would also recommend.

Bernard Lewis
2001 *The Middle East: 2000 Years of History from the rise of Christianity to the present day.*
UK: Weidenfeld and Nicholson

Fascinating history, reminding us of the Arab World's Islamic and earlier Christian heritage.

2002 *What Went Wrong? The Clash between Islam and Modernity in the Middle East*
UK: Phoenix

A bestseller, highlighting the achievements of the Islamic empires and explaining something of the pain now being felt across the Arab World.

John L Esposito
2003 *Unholy War: Terror in the Name of Islam?*
USA: Oxford University Press, Inc

Cool-headed analysis from a long-standing scholar of political Islam, respected for his scholarship both among Muslims and in the West.

Albert Hourani
2002 *A History of the Arab Peoples*
UK: Faber and Faber

Still the classic. A wonderful book.

Books from a particularly Christian perspective:

Robin Daniel
1993 *This Holy Seed*
UK: Tamarisk Publications.

Detailed history of the North African church written from a North African evangelical perspective. Available from WEC Publications, Bulstrode, Oxford Rd, Gerrards Cross, Bucks, SL9 8SZ.

Christine A Mallouhi
2002 *Waging Peace on Islam*
UK: IVP

Takes St Francis of Assisi as an example of how Christians ought to share the gospel with Muslims.

WEBSITES

Hard news of hidden Christians in the Arab World rarely makes it to a location as public as a website; for specific prayer information you need to subscribe to confidential mailing lists. The following sites, however, are all helpful.

www.amnesty.org and www.hrw.org
Home pages of Amnesty International and Human Rights Watch, large international human rights organizations.

www.awm.org
Informative site of Arab World Ministries who recruit expatriates to serve in the Arab World.

www.barnabasfund.org
Home page of a ministry to the persecuted Church with some news links.

www.christianmonitor.org
Well-organized site that gathers headlines of persecution against Christians.

www.coptic.net
Introduction to the Egyptian Orthodox Church.

www.copticpope.net
In English: but if you speak Arabic, you can download or watch his latest lecture.

www.highway-projects.org
Short-term, practical mission work, usually among disadvantaged people from the Arab community, across the religious divide, in fellowship with established Arab Christian congregations.

www.holylandtrust.org
American-based charity working towards 'strengthening and improving the lives' of people in the Middle East. Some very helpful materials here and also on their associated website www.middleeastwindow.com *which is an online journal for 'thoughtful Christians rediscovering the Middle East.'*

www.jerusalem.anglican.org
Brief information about Arab World Anglicans.

www.rediscoveringpalestine.org.uk
UK-based network of charities working towards 'peace with justice in Palestine and Israel'.

www.sat7.org
News of the satellite broadcaster.

NOTES

CHAPTER 1

1   Acts 2:10-11. Libya was the Roman province that included northern Egypt as well as some of present-day Libya. 'Arabs' probably refers to a tribe who inhabited what is now Jordan.

2   Tertullian *To Scapula 2*, quoted in Robin Daniel *This Holy Seed*, Tamarisk publications, 1993, p 63. (Note, though, that Tertullian was prone to exaggerate!)

3   Gabriel Camps *Berbères aux Marges de l'Histoire* (Editions des Hespérides, 1980) quoted in Robin Daniel *This Holy Seed*, Tamarisk publications, 1993, p 64.

4   Robin Daniel *This Holy Seed*, Tamarisk publications, 1993, p 178.

5   F J Foakes-Jackson *History of the Christian Church to AD 461* (Cambridge, UK; J D Hall and Son, 1909), quoted by Robin Daniel *This Holy Seed*, Tamarisk publications, 1993, p 18.

6   Walzer, R *Greek into Arabic* (Oxford, 1962), p 12, quoted by Albert Hourani: *A History of the Arab Peoples*, Faber & Faber 1991, p 76.

7   Albert Hourani (*A History of the Arab Peoples*, Faber & Faber 1991, p 78) attributes the following to 'A famous medical writer of the ninth century, Abu Bakr al-Razi (865-925)': 'Human reason alone could give certain knowledge, the path of philosophy was open to all uses, the claims of revelation were false and religions were dangerous.'

8   John L Esposito *The Islamic Threat: Myth or Reality*, second edition OUP New York 1995, p 415.

9   Kenneth Cragg *The Arab Christian, A History in the Middle East*, Mobrays: London 1992, p 18.

10 Albert Hourani *A History of the Arab Peoples*, Faber & Faber 1991, p 96.

11 Robin Daniel *This Holy Seed*, Tamarisk Publications, UK, 1995, p 420.

12 Albert Hourani *A History of the Arab Peoples*, Faber & Faber 1991, p 47.

13 Bernard Lewis *The Middle East*, London, Weidenfeld & Nicholson 1995, p 261.

14 Though not perhaps as an Arab – Arab imperial power was already on the wane in the tenth century.

15 Kenneth Cragg, *The Arab Christian, A History in the Middle East*, Mowbrays, London 1992, p 118.

16 Bernard Lewis *The Middle East*, London, Weidenfeld & Nicholson 1995, p 115.

CHAPTER 2

17 *Silihdar Tarihi* (Istanbul 1928), Vol II, p 87, quoted in Bernard Lewis *The Middle East*, London: Weidenfeld and Nicholson 1995, p 277.

18 Bernard Lewis *The Middle East*, London, Weidenfeld & Nicholson 1995, p 288.

19 Albert Hourani *A History of the Arab Peoples*, Faber & Faber 1991, p 281-282.

20 *The Guardian* 4th November 1995, reviewing historian Elizabeth Monroe's book *Britain's Moment in the Middle East*.

21 Albert Hourani *A History of the Arab Peoples*, Faber & Faber 1991, p 442.

22 R T Abed in *Middle East International*, no. 470, 4th March 1994, pages 20-21.

23 Bernard Lewis *The Middle East*, London, Weidenfeld & Nicholson 1995, p 7.

24 See *The Economist*, November 2,2002.

25 The name for the status classical Islam gives to non-Muslim minorities within a Muslim state.

26 2 Corinthians 8: 1-2.

27 Christine Mallouhi *Mini-Skirts, Mothers and Muslims*, Spear Publications 1996, UK p 93 and 94. Used with permission.

CHAPTER 3

28 See *'A faith on the verge of extinction'* by Khalid Amayreh, published on April 26th 2004 on the al-Jazeera website, english.aljazeera.net.

29 Arab World Ministries *Update* (1995), No. 2.

CHAPTER 4

30 *The Economist*, October 17 2002.

31 AP report, Feb 28 2002.

32 Bin Laden tape reported by BBC Monitoring, Feb 16th 2003.

33 See for example, *The Economist*, June 27 2002.

34 Ziauddin Sardar and Zafar Abbas Malik, *Introducing Islam* (Cambridge, UK: Icon Books) 1994, p 160.

35 You can read more about the Holy Land Trust – 'a non-profit humanitarian organization dedicated to strengthening and improving the lives of children, families and communities in the Middle East' – and access some of their resources via their site www.holylandtrust.org.

CHAPTER 5

36 This is the conclusion of Mansour Khalid, a former Sudanese foreign minister, in his book *War and Peace in the Sudan: a tale of two countries*, (Keegan Paul 2003), among others.

37 The documentary is *Sudan: the Hidden Holocaust*, available from The Persecution Project foundation (www.persecutionproject.org).

38 See for example the Human Rights Watch website, www.hrw.org.

39 See for example, Compass direct report dated April 28 2004 *Sudan: Islamic law imposed on Khartoum's southerners*. (www compassdirect.org)

40 See Stan Guthrie *Hope Amid the Ruins* in *Christianity Today*, January 2004.

41 According to Makram Morgos, Executive Secretary of the Bible Society in Sudan, press release dated 30 August 2000. (See the Bible Societies' Opportunity 21 website www.o-21.org.)

42 See the press release *Sudan: Revival amidst unspeakable horror* issued by the World Evangelical Alliance on June 5 2002. (www.worldevangelical.org)

CHAPTER 6

43 Quoted on a visit in July 1994 (he was referring primarily to the Holy Land but the comment stands for the whole region).

44 Newsbrief from the mission agency Open Doors, Feb 1995; *Operation World*, 2001.

45 From a conversation with missions researcher Patrick Johnstone, April 1995.

46 Open Doors *Newsbrief*, February 1995.
47 By which I mean people who respect Christian festivals and morals, and who see themselves as part of the Christian community, but who do not necessarily lay claim to a living relationship with Christ.
48 For a sympathetic treatment of Orthodoxy from an evangelical viewpoint see Daniel B Clendenin *Why I'm not Orthodox* in *Christianity Today*, January 6th 1997, pp 32-38.
49 Athanasios S Frangopoulos *Our Orthodox Christian Faith, a handbook of popular dogmatics*. The Brotherhood of Theologians 'O Sotir' ('The Saviour'), Athens, March 1993, p 169.
50 Athanasios S Frangopoulos *Our Orthodox Christian Faith, a handbook of popular dogmatics*. The Brotherhood of Theologians "O Sotir" ("The Saviour"), Athens, March 1993, p 169.
51 Egyptian diplomat and Orthodox Christian Boutros Ghali.
52 Anglican Bishop Michael Nazir-Ali, former head of the Church Missionary Society, quoted in *The Independent*, 4th January 1994.

CHAPTER 7
53 Luke 21:16.
54 John 16:2.
55 Personal letter to author, June 2004.
56 Wendell Evans, quoted in the AWM video *Against the Tide*.
57 Letter to the author, May 2004.
58 Interview with the author, March 2004.
59 This is an estimate supplied by an Algerian Berber. No-one knows the real figure: counting Berbers was a priority neither of the French nor the Algerian governments. Historically it is beyond doubt that most Algerians are Berbers.
60 From a personal interview with two Berber Christians in Paris, September 1996.

FOR PRAYER

- For Arab World governments, that they will be just, wise and full of integrity. For them to protect minorities and religious freedoms.

- For a just settlement and for reconciliation between Israel and the Arab World.

- For the Christian communities, local and expatriate, of the Arab World. For Christ to be known, loved and worshipped among them. For a growth in brotherly love. For endurance.

- For God's blessing on the enemies of the gospel within the Arab World – that they would know Christ, his love, his redemptive power.

- For the youth of the Arab World to find their hope in Christ.

- For the Arab World's poor, handicapped, and outcast.

- For the foreign ministries that aim to bring the gospel to the Arab World, that they would be humble-minded, sensitive, loving, and effective.